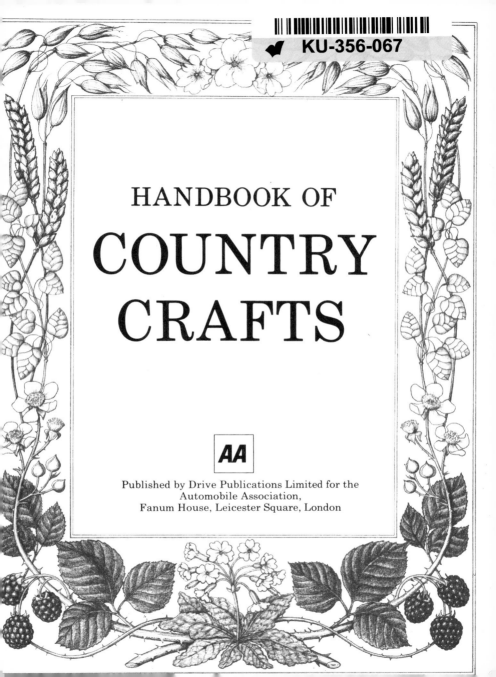

HANDBOOK OF

COUNTRY

CRAFTS

AA

Published by Drive Publications Limited for the
Automobile Association,
Fanum House, Leicester Square, London

The publishers express their gratitude for contributions by
the following people:

Consultant Editor   Barbara Hargreaves

Writers   Janet Barber
                       Suzanne M. Beedell
                       Marjorie Haines
                       Gordon A. Message
                       Joyce Thomas

Artists   Ann Evans
                       The Garden Studio (Gwen Simpson)
                       Scenographica
                       (Julian Holland, Mike Cussens)

Others   Dried plants and flowers supplied by
                       Peter Harvey Co. Ltd, High Wycombe

Handbook of Country Crafts
was edited and designed by Drive Publications Limited,
Berkeley Square House, London W1X 5PD
for the Automobile Association,
Fanum House, Basingstoke, Hants RG21 2EA.

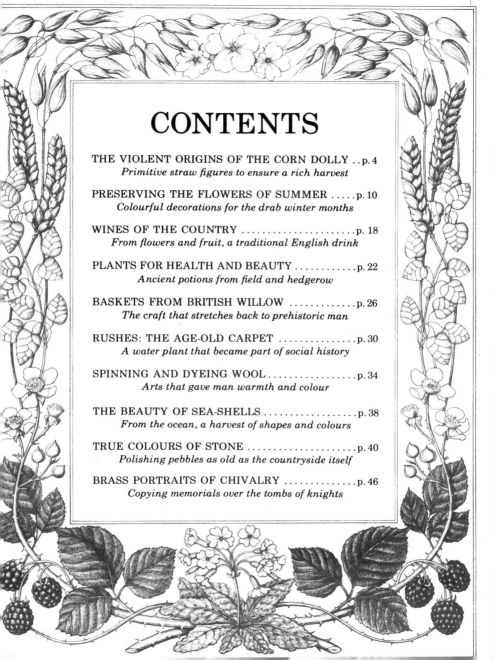

CONTENTS

The violent origins of the corn dolly

The intricately woven straw decorations that brighten churches throughout Britain at the time of Harvest Festival have their origins not in the Christian religion but in beliefs and ideas stretching back into pre-history.

The celebration of the harvest is steeped in legend and mythology, and centres around the story of Ceres, the Earth Mother, goddess of all that grows out of the earth.

It is still the custom in some areas for farmers to leave a row of wheat standing in the fields at the end of the harvest in the belief that bad luck will befall them if it is cut. The legend is that Ceres hides in the corn. In some parts of Northamptonshire, until the

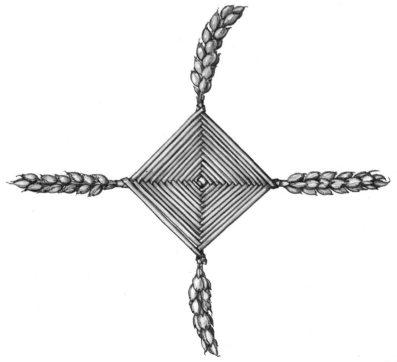

The Bridget Cross is an Irish version of the corn dollies that decorate churches at harvest time. Their origins stretch back to pagan worship of Ceres, the Earth Mother

early 1900's, a sheaf of corn would be left in the fields, and while it stood there no one was allowed to go into the field. When the sheaf was taken out, women and children were allowed to enter and glean through the stubble.

In another part of the country the last row of corn used to be beaten down to the ground by the reapers shouting 'There she is!' 'Hit her!' 'Knock her into the ground!' 'Don't let her get away!' This way the spirit of the corn mother was driven into the earth to remain until the next year.

It is out of these beliefs that there grew the tradition of preserving the last stalks of corn from a field and making them into the shape of a woman adorned with gay ribbons, usually blue. This figure – the corn dolly – was then carried to the farmhouse and displayed on the wall during the harvest festivities. In most areas, the dolly was kept safely until the sowing of the seeds in the following spring.

The very name of the straw decorations varies from one part of the country and from one part of the world to another. It is known as corn mother,

THE SIMPLEST CORN DOLLY—A BRIDGET CROSS

Tools: scissors or knife
Materials: 2 thick straws; several thinner (weaver) straws (see p. 6), buff-colour thread; 4 heads of wheat

1 Decide the size, from corner to corner, of the cross to be made. Cut two thick pieces to that length from the base of the straw

2 Cut several pieces of weaving straw. Cut them just above the top leaf node, and trim off the reeds

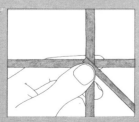

3 Hold the thick straws in a cross shape, with the thin end of a weaver straw laid diagonally over the centre

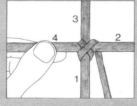

4 Wind the weaver straw behind 1 and back over the centre to bend down behind 2

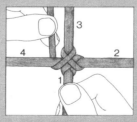

5 Wind the straw up across the centre. Bend it behind 3, cross over the centre and up behind 4. Continue in that order – 1, 2, 3 & 4

6 When a new piece of weaver is needed, hold the old straw against one of the arms of the cross and cut it neatly. Push the thin end of the new weaver straw into the thicker end of the old weaver

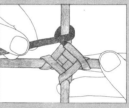

7 Twist the new weaver around the back of the arm and across the front to hide and secure the join. Continue weaving until the Bridget Cross is complete

8 Finish by twisting the weaver three times around the nearest arm of the cross and tie securely with a piece of buff-coloured thread

9 Cut four good heads of wheat with 4 in. of stem. Push the stems into the ends of the arms of the cross

mell baby, corn baby, kirn child, kirn dolly and mell mother. The derivation of the word dolly has been attributed to the similarity of the straw figure to a child's doll. It seems more likely, however, to be a corruption over many centuries of the word 'idol'.

One of the most gruesome harvest-time rituals was practised in central Asia Minor between the Mediter-

The Nek dolly is a solid column of straw originating from an ancient ritual in Asia Minor. Phrygian farmers would capture a

- Weaver straw

- Thick straw for Bridget cross

Straw for dollies can be wheat, rye, barley or oats, but wheat is best. Weaving straw is cut just above the first leaf node, and should be used within a few days

A NEK DOLLY—STEP BY STEP

Tools: scissors or knife
Materials: 18 straws with heads; several straws without heads; buff-coloured thread; elastic band; ribbons

1 Cut 18 weaver straws, complete with good heads, from just above the first leaf node (see drawing on the left). Cut several more straws without heads. (Alternatively, you can make the dolly by using ordinary drinking straws)

2 Arrange the 18 straws in a bundle and tie with buff thread close to the heads

straws equally spaced around the bundle and spread them outwards from the thread binding. Wrap an elastic band or thread around the remaining bundle about an inch from the end. With a ball-point pen or a pencil, number each of the five straws 1–5 anti-clockwise

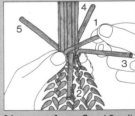

4 Lay straw 1 over 2 and 3 to lie between 3 and 4. Turn the bundle a quarter-turn clockwise after each weave

5 Lay straw 3 over 1 and 4 to lie between 4 and 5

3 Hold the bundle with the heads downwards. Select five

ranean Sea and the Black Sea, where the Phrygians, a cattle-raising and agricultural people, worshipped Cybele, the mother of the gods. These primitive people, who contributed

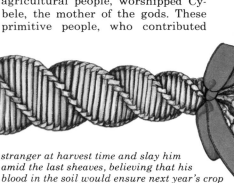

stranger at harvest time and slay him amid the last sheaves, believing that his blood in the soil would ensure next year's crop

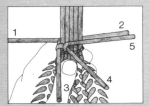

6 Lay 4 over 3 and 5. Lay 5 over 4 to lie alongside 2

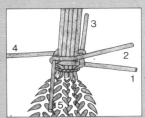

7 Take 2 back under 5 and up over 5 to lie between 1 and 3

8 Lay 1 over 2 and 3, 3 over 1 and 4, 4 over 3 and 5, 5 over 4 and 2, 2 over 5 and 1. Now continue weaving in this order

9 When each straw is almost used, cut it over the corner of the last completed weave. Push the thin end of a new straw into the existing straw. Now continue the weaving

10 When the dolly is almost the length required, trim the ends of the bundle. Continue weaving to cover the straws in the core. Steadily bring the weave in closer and closer

11 Make sure that the weavers are at least 8 in. long when the weaving has closed up. If necessary, add new weavers to provide the extra length

12 Continue weaving closely almost to the end of the weavers, creating a rope-like handle for the dolly

13 Bend the 'rope' into a loop, gently pull the strands of the dolly apart, and insert the end straws of the loop. This method of finishing off can be tricky, and a simpler alternative is explained under drop dolly overleaf (p. 9)

14 Decorate with ribbons

The drop dolly, the traditional corn-dolly shape, is the most difficult to make. The technique of weaving is similar to that for the Nek, but the drop dolly is hollow

many oriental ideas to the early Greeks, practised a ceremony called crying the Nek at harvest time.

The Nek is a column of straw plaited with about five strands to form a thick pole-like dolly. It originates from the Phrygian custom of taking captive any stranger who happened to be near the corn fields when the harvesting was taking place. Their belief was that the corn spirit of the earth entered the stranger's body.

The ritual that followed was intended to satisfy the dictates of the legend that the corn spirit must go back to earth. The victim was placed in the middle of the last sheaves of corn that had been cut and these were placed about him. His head was then cut off with sickles. The blood that spilt into the earth was supposed to contain the spirit of the corn, thus ensuring grace in the eyes of the gods for the following year.

A much milder version of crying the Nek was practised in this country in the Devon area until about 150 years ago. The Nek dolly was formed from the last row of wheat and all the reapers formed a circle. The dolly was held so that the ears of the wheat pointed uppermost. Each reaper in turn bowed to the centre of the circle and touched the ears of wheat to the ground to ensure that the corn spirit remained in the earth.

The most widely known corn-dolly shape – the drop dolly – is similar in technique to the Nek dolly, except that the Nek has a core of straws while the drop dolly is hollow.

From Ireland we have inherited a variation that is used often as a decoration on the traditional dollies. This straw work – called the Bridget Cross – is the simplest to make.

HOW TO MAKE A TRADITIONAL DROP DOLLY

Tools: scissors or knife
Materials: 5 long straws with heads; several straws without heads; buff-coloured thread; ribbon

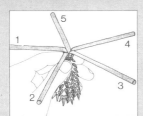

1 Cut five long pieces of weaver straw, complete with heads, just above the first leaf node (see p. 6). Tie with buff-coloured thread just above the heads and spread out the straws. With a ball-point pen or a pencil, number the straws anti-clockwise 1–5

2 Hold the heads carefully in one hand and lay straw 1 across 2 and 3 to lie between 3 and 4. Turn straws quarter-turn clockwise

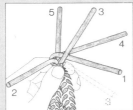

3 Lay 3 across 1 and 4. Lay 4 across 3 and 5. Lay 5 across 4 and 2

4 Lay 2 across 5 to lie parallel to 1

5 Take 1 under 2 and bend over 2 so that it lies parallel with 3

6 Take 3 under and over 1, so that it lies parallel to 4. Continue the operation with successive straws

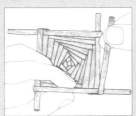

7 As the weave widens, change the position of the hands so that the woven shape can be held securely

8 When a weaver is almost used, cut it against the corner of the weave. Push a new thin end of weaver straw into the old weaver

9 When the dolly is about half the length required, start to decrease its width by slightly overlapping the straws as you weave instead of laying them parallel

10 Near the end, make sure that at least three straws will be 8 in. long when the weave is closed. Cut and add new weavers if necessary to give that length

11 When the weave is complete, bend the straws upwards and tie securely with buff-coloured thread; plait the three longest straws

12 Bend the plait into a loop and tie it to the two remaining straws close to the end of the woven dolly. Trim off the surplus two straws. Decorate with ribbon

Preserving the flowers of summer

Of all the crafts associated with the country one of the most delightful is the preservation and display of flowers, foliage and fruit.

Blossoms picked in high summer and leaves gathered during autumn can be pressed and used to make beautiful collage pictures. Or larger flowers and sprays of leaves can be preserved in a near-natural state by drying. Bunches of dried flowers make really beautiful winter decorations.

For pressing, always gather flowers, grasses, seed heads and leaves when they are dry, otherwise mould will form. When leaves are found on roads after a high wind and they need to be washed, dry them with an absorbent kitchen towel before they are pressed.

Press all the collected material as soon as possible after gathering. Special flower presses are available at craft shops, but there is little reason why the beginner cannot obtain good results with traditional methods.

Prepare leaves, flowers and seeds separately for pressing, and always discard any thick stalks.

Have available enough sheets of blotting paper and a considerable number of heavy books or ordinary bricks to weigh down the flowers and plants during pressing.

To get the best results it is often

Key to pressed flowers

A *Fool's parsley leaf*
B *Ground elder flower*
C *Hares tail*
D *Fern*
E *Mimosa*
F *Grevillea robusta*
G *Freesia*
H *Sycamore*
I *Larkspur*
J *Rhodanthe*
K *Delphinium*
L *Russian vine*
M *Senecio maritima*
N *Raspberry leaf*
O *Blackberry leaf*
P *Chamomile leaf*
Q *Red currant leaf (reversed)*
R *Acrolinium*

Delicate pictures can be made from almost any pressed flowers, leaves or grasses. The background may be plain cardboard, or rich materials such as silk, velvet or tweed

necessary to peel off the petals – for example with roses – and press each singly. Only after the petals have been pressed should they be reassembled as a flower. A common daisy can be used as the centre piece of a mock rose.

Each little stalk of golden rod and mimosa should be pressed separately.

With daffodils, remove the thick seed box under the head and slit the flower carefully down the middle with a razor blade. This gives two 'flowers' of three petals and half a trumpet for each pressing.

When the coloured petals are delicate – for example, the poppy – always lay two petals on top of each other. This will give them a deeper colour.

If a flower has a very thick centre, like the marigold, press the centre firmly with the thumb before laying it on to the blotting paper.

When the stalks of a flower have to be discarded because they are too thick for pressing, use instead those of primrose, clover or clematis.

Some flowers, foliage and grasses are particularly suitable for pressing. FLOWERS Acrolinium, buttercup, clematis, daisy, delphinium, larkspur, golden rod, mimosa, hydrangea florets, lobelia, montbretia and pansy.

CREATING A PRESSED-FLOWER PICTURE

Tools: small paint brush; scissors; hammer
Materials: pressed flowers; picture frame with glass; hardboard to fit frame; cardboard or other background material; practice paper; brown paper; latex adhesive such as Copydex or Jiffytex; tacks

1 Cut a piece of background material and practice paper to the size required

2 Lay out a selection of the pressed flowers. Avoid too much handling. Use a small paint brush to move them around the paper

3 Build up the pattern of the picture to suit the pressings available. Always retain the natural curve of any stalks and grasses, and avoid putting too many pressed flowers into one pattern

4 Raspberry leaves give good visual weight at the base of the picture. Keep small and delicate material to the top and edges to avoid a top-heavy appearance

5 When the arrangement is satisfactory, gently dab a little latex adhesive on the centre of the flower with the tip of the brush handle

6 For stalks and leaves, dab a little adhesive in several places along their length

7 Gently press into position with the fingers

8 When the picture is complete press the glass down over it and leave to dry

9 Fix the whole arrangement into the frame with the hardboard backing. Secure with tacks. Cover the back completely with brown paper to protect from moths and dust

Even the much-hated garden weed ground elder may be used for pressing – with its pretty florets, black seed head and fern-like leaf.

LEAVES Ferns, *Grevillea robusta*, epimedium, beech, ivy, clematis, senecio maritima, centaurea, achillea, maple.

GRASSES Barley, quaking grass, hares tail and fairy grass.

Most yellow and orange flowers press well and retain their colour – especially montbretia, daffodil and marigold. Rhodanthe, acrolinium, cosmos and larkspur give good white, pink and mauve colours. Delphinium, larkspur and lobelia give blue.

Ivy turns to many shades of brown according to the variety. The grey leaves of centaurea and cineraria are beautiful with pink, white and mauve flowers, and they never change colour. Raspberry and aspen can be used to reveal their grey side. Beech turns to brown, red or gold. *Cobaea scandens* (cathedral bell), has leaves that turn mauve with purple veins in November.

How to press
Lay the flowers, leaves or grasses between sheets of blotting paper in a book with absorbent pages. (Don't use your most treasured book.) Weigh down with other books or with bricks.

Alternatively, put the flowers between sheets of newspaper and lay them under a carpet.

Most leaves and some flowers take between three and four weeks to dry.

Do not be tempted to remove the weights too soon. Leave for at least four weeks, and for longer if on the first inspection they seem not to be ready. Inspect flowers with thick centres often during the pressing, and renew blotting paper if damp.

Once the flowers are ready they can be used to make a picture. Beginners may choose to work on black, white or coloured cardboard, but hessian and velvet, slub linen, silk and even tweed are highly regarded by experts.

The material must be large enough to allow a good overlap with the wood backing to which it will be fixed later.

Have available a duplicate piece of material, or a sheet of paper, so that the pressed flowers, leaves or grasses may be laid out in a practice design before being glued.

Personal cards from leaf skeletons
An unusual and attractive way of preserving leaves is to make leaf-skeleton pictures – or personal greetings cards to send to friends.

The first step is to remove all the soft vegetable matter from the leaf, leaving only the skeleton.

Obtain six large cabbage leaves. Put in a saucepan and add 2 pints of water. Bring to the boil and simmer for half an hour. Strain off the liquid into a bucket and allow to cool. Make sure that the leaves to be treated are in good condition and place them in the cabbage water. It is advisable to place the bucket of water a good distance from the house. After a few days the liquid begins to smell.

Examine the leaves after a week and gently turn them in the liquid.

Inspect them regularly and when the vegetable matter has softened considerably remove them from the bucket and rinse them very gently in clean water. Use a soft-bristled paint brush to dislodge any remaining leaf material.

An alternative way to remove the leaf material is to use washing soda. Dissolve a dessertspoon of soda to each pint of water, heat to below boiling point, remove from the heat and soak the leaves for about an hour. Brush away the rotting material.

Be careful not to get the soda in the eyes or on the skin.

Place the leaf skeleton on a piece of clean newspaper and leave in an airing cupboard to dry.

When it is dry the leaf skeleton will

Leaf skeletons are made by removing all the soft material from a leaf, leaving only the veins, which can be used for decoration

be a dirty brown colour. Lay it gently in a very dilute solution of bleach and water. After a few hours remove it from the bleach, lay it on newspaper and allow to dry.

The leaf skeleton may then be used to make a decorative card or picture.

If required, the skeleton can be coloured in a vegetable dye.

To prepare a picture, spread a thin film of glue over a piece of plate glass or thick Perspex. Lay the leaf skeleton carefully on to the glued surface. Lift the two together carefully, turn over and position on a suitable background card. Gently press flat and allow to dry. Press if necessary.

Techniques for drying flowers

A rewarding pastime on a country holiday is to gather flowers and seed heads for drying into home displays. There are several methods of drying, and the simplest require no equipment.

Some flowers dry naturally if left standing in water in a warm room until the water has evaporated – for example delphiniums, larkspur, golden rod, bells of Ireland and hydrangea. Make sure, however, that hydrangea heads feel leathery to the fingers before trying to dry them.

Another simple method is air-drying, which works well for delphiniums, larkspur, helichrysum, rhodanthe, sea lavender and Chinese lanterns. Seed heads such as teasels, foxgloves, gladioli, poppy heads, iris pods, barley, oats, quaking grass and hares tail all respond well to air-drying.

Always gather flowers when they are dry and not too mature, so that the colour is strong. Remove all the leaves and hang the flowers in small bunches in a dry airy place protected from direct sunlight.

Borax may be used to preserve flowers, and its advantage is that it heightens and preserves their colour. A disadvantage is that it makes the flowers more fragile than air-drying.

Use this method for flower heads of roses, French marigolds, and rhodanthe. Place the flower heads in a cardboard box on a layer of powdered borax. Cover completely with borax. Replace the lid and leave in an airing cupboard. When dry, carefully place a fine hooked stub wire, obtainable from a florists' supplier, through the head to provide a stem.

Inspect the flowers after 48 hours, but do not remove them until they are papery to the touch – which in

Seeds and grasses make unusual hanging decorations, and sycamore seeds are a good basis for a propeller design. The seedbuds are split, pointed and glued over a small cardboard disc. A small larch cone and feathery grasses complete the decoration

some cases can take up to ten days.

Probably one of the most successful and rewarding ways to preserve foliage and seed heads – such as old man's beard and sorrel – is to stand them in a mixture of glycerine and water.

Beech, maple, oak, berberis and other deciduous leaves can also be preserved this way, but they should be treated when young, never when changing colour. Remove all the unwanted, discoloured leaves and slit the stem up about $\frac{1}{2}$ in. from the bottom.

Pour 1 part glycerine to 2 parts hot water into a sturdy jar or wide-mouthed jug and stir thoroughly. Stand the stems in the liquid.

Beech leaves change colour after 10 to 14 days. Inspect the leaves frequently and make sure that they do not become saturated with the glycerine mixture. If liquid begins to ooze out of the leaves remove them from the mixture, wipe them thoroughly and store in a dry airy place.

Evergreen leaves – for example Portugal laurel and ivy – produce rich dark brown colours when preserved this way.

A simple way to prevent dried wild fruit from dropping is to spray them with an ordinary hair spray. Try this with rose hips, hawthorn haws, spindle berries, honeysuckle or holly.

Arranging dried flowers

Knead a suitable amount of plasticine, dry oasis foam (obtainable from a florist), or any other special material available from craft shops. Place the base material in a container and criss-cross it with strong rubber bands. Push the ends of the dried plants into the base material to give the desired arrangement.

Key to dried plants

A   *Bells of Ireland*
B   *Teasels*
C   *Poppy seed heads*
D   *Pampas grass*
E   *Beech leaves*
F   *Achillea*
G   *Fern*
H   *Golden rod*
I   *Chinese lanterns*
J   *Oats*
K   *Barley*
L   *Hares tail*
M   *Oak leaves*
N   *Aspidistra leaf*
O   *Quaking grass*
P   *Hydrangea*

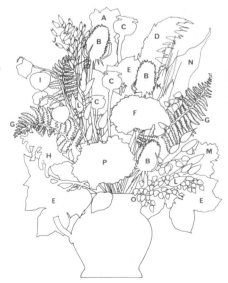

Dried grasses, leaves and seed heads, massed in a large jug or vase, make a varied and colourful winter display. No equipment is needed for the simplest drying techniques

17

Wines of the country

Wine can be made from almost any non-poisonous flower, fruit, leaf or root plant. Many recipes suggest a large variety of ingredients and special yeasts and slightly varying methods, but the secret of successful wine-making, until you are experienced, is to keep the process simple.

Really excellent wines can be made by following very simple rules.

Always pick fruit when it is ripe but not mushy, flowers when they are out but not overblown, and leaves when they are young. Gather them in dry weather, preferably in sunshine. Wash in water and dry. Remove unwanted leaves and stalks and use the fruit or plants at once.

Some fruits, such as apples and plums, release pectin when boiling water is poured on to them. This makes the wine difficult to clear at a later stage. To counteract this a teaspoonful of pectic enzyme is added to each gallon of liquid at the early stage.

At every stage of wine-making it is important to keep the liquid covered or corked, and to exclude fresh air from it as far as possible. Fresh air oxidises wine and ruins the taste.

When using citrus fruits to make wine, never allow any of the white pith of the skin to get into the wine. It gives a bitter taste.

Keep everything very clean. Use Campden tablets dissolved in water to sterilise bottles and jars before use. Leave the Campden and water solution in the jar for at least a few hours.

One of the most useful tools for the home wine-maker is a wine hydrometer (obtainable from a chemist) which measures the amount of sugar in the wine. If the finished wine is too dry it can be sweetened by adding sugar – provided that it is well dissolved. If a wine is found to be too sweet, the only solution is to blend it with a drier home-made wine.

When wine has not cleared even after several months it can be improved by adding liquid finings or

4 pint saucepan

Polythene bucket with lid

Plastic strainer

1½ in. corks

Measuring jug

Wooden mallet

Wooden spoon

Equipment for making country wines exists largely in any kitchen, and the rest can be

more pectic enzyme. But most wine will clear if it is left long enough.

The wine should be stored in bottles, lying on their sides, for at least four months before drinking.

Wine which is bottled while still fermenting slightly – and this can happen even after several months of maturing – will sparkle when it is uncorked. This can make it most enjoyable, but there is a risk that the pressure of carbon dioxide gas that builds up will blow out the cork. When sparkling wine is deliberately being made it is best to bottle it in Champagne bottles and tie down the corks with wires that can be bought.

The following are the British wild plants most commonly used for wine-making. (They are illustrated in colour on pp. 22–25.) Just follow the basic recipe in the panel overleaf, incorporating any additional ingredients that are specified there.

BILBERRIES (blueberries, whortleberries) Mash well; add pectic enzyme.

BLACKBERRIES Do not mash. Squeeze the fruit gently by hand.

BLACKTHORN BERRIES (sloe) Mash well.

COWSLIP FLOWERS Remove green parts

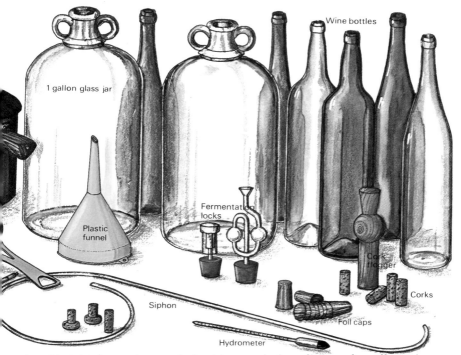

Labels within image: Wine bottles, 1 gallon glass jar, Plastic funnel, Fermentation locks, Cork flogger, Corks, Siphon, Foil caps, Hydrometer

bought at hardware shops and chemists. Almost any flowers and fruits can be the main ingredient, and excellent wines are made with the simplest possible methods

19

of the flower heads, add juice and grated rind of two oranges.

DANDELION FLOWERS Remove green parts. Add juice and grated rind of two oranges.

ELDER FLOWERS Shred florets from the large heads. To make sparkling wine, bottle it as soon as it has cleared.

ELDERBERRIES (known as the 'English Grape') Mash well.

FENNEL Use one large handful of fennel and 3 lb. beetroot. Boil the cleaned and sliced beetroot in 6 pints of water until tender, strain the liquid on to the sugar. Pour 2 pints of boiling water over the fennel and leave for a day. Mix the strained liquids and follow basic recipe.

HAWTHORN BERRIES Mash well. Add juice and grated rind of two oranges.

HAWTHORN BLOSSOM (or May blossom)

NETTLES Add ½ oz. root ginger.

PRIMROSE FLOWERS Add juice and grated rind of two oranges. Remove

---

THE CHEAPEST WAY TO STOCK A WINE CELLAR

Ingredients
3–4 lb. berries or fruit or
3–4 pints blossoms or leaves
2½–3 lb. sugar
½ oz. dried baker's yeast
Juice and grated rind of 1 lemon
1 cupful cold tea
1 gallon water
½ teaspoonful yeast nutrient and pectic enzyme if required (both available from a chemist)

Equipment
The basic equipment is obtainable from a good chemist or ironmonger. It consists of:
Two 1 gallon glass jars
1½ in. cork
1½ in. cork with a hole in it
Fermentation lock
Polythene bucket with lid
Plastic funnel
Plastic strainer
Plastic or wooden spoon
Wooden mallet
4 pint saucepan
4 ft rubber or polythene tubing
Six wine bottles and corks
Plastic caps
Cork flogger
Hydrometer
Filter bag
Campden tablets

Making a 'must'
1 Put fruit or flowers into the bucket and pour in 4 pints of boiling water to make a 'must'. Add 1 teaspoonful of pectic enzyme if required. Stir, mash well with a mallet, and cover with the lid

2 Next day, stir and mash again. Cover; leave for a day

Straining the liquid

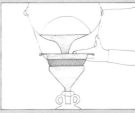

3 On the third day, pour through a strainer into a 1 gallon glass jar. If the fruit is very mushy, use a filter or jelly bag. Add 1 cup of cold tea and the fruit juice and grated rind.

4 Put the sugar into a saucepan and just cover with water. Bring to boil and stir until dissolved. Allow to cool and add to the jar. Add boiled water to bring the

level of the must to within 3 in. from the top of the jar

5 Float the wine hydrometer in the must and take a reading according to the manufacturer's instructions. If the wine is still not sweet enough, dissolve some more sugar in water and add to the jar

6 When the jar feels just warm to the hand, pour off ½ cupful of must and stir the yeast and yeast nutrient into it. After about half an hour add the yeast mixture to the jar

7 Plug the jar lightly with a wad of cotton wool. Leave to stand in a normally heated room for at least two days

Corking the jar

8 When the fermentation has become less fierce (about the

as much of the green material as possible from the primrose flowers.

Home-made liqueurs

Liqueurs can also be made at home by soaking fruit in spirits such as gin or brandy. The method is practically foolproof as the alcohol inhibits fermentation and the fruit cannot go bad.

Traditional liqueurs are made from: sloes, plus four or five blanched almonds, in gin; blackberries, plus two cloves and a small piece of cinnamon, in brandy; and hawthorn blossom in brandy.

Half fill a large preserving jar with the fruit or blossom, add $\frac{1}{2}$ lb. white sugar and enough spirit to fill the jar up to the lid. Shake the jar, put it on a shelf and reverse it at least twice a week. After two months, bottle the liquid (there will be more than you started with), and use the fruit in a jelly topped up with whipped cream.

---

third day), remove the cotton wool and fit a cork and fermentation lock (there are two types, both equally efficient)

Topping up
9 After two more days, top up to within $1\frac{1}{2}$ in. of the cork with boiled water. Leave to stand until fermentation has stopped and no bubbles are rising

Racking

10 It is now time to 'rack' the wine to separate it from the sediment. Place the jar on a table and position a second jar at a lower level near by. Insert a siphon tube in the top jar and suck gently. When the wine starts to flow, place the free end of the tube in the lower jar. Allow all the wine to run into the second jar, but take care not to disturb or suck up the sediment in the first jar

11 Cork the new jar tightly and store it in a cool place with an even temperature for two months

Second racking
12 After two months, repeat the siphoning. Re-cork and leave for about three months

Bottling
13 Check the condition of the wine occasionally. When it is completely clear, prepare to bottle it

14 Soak the corks for the bottles in hot water for an hour

15 Make sure that the bottles are clean and siphon the wine into them. Do not disturb any remaining sediment

16 Push a cork into the flogger. Hold a bottle firmly and place the flogger on top of it. Press the plunger, or hammer with a wooden mallet, until the cork is fully home

17 Store the bottles on their sides for as long as possible, but for at least four months before drinking the wine

18 Labels and plastic caps from chemists complete the appearance of the bottles and provide a record of the contents

Plants for health and beauty

Almost every plant, poisonous or not, once had some cosmetic or medicinal use, which our ancestors understood well before the development of the chemicals industry. Herbal teas and syrups were used as general tonics or as remedies for specific complaints, such as catarrh or insomnia. Herbal cosmetics were used to clean and freshen the skin.

Herbal recipes use some of Britain's most common plants, such as blackberries, dandelions and hawthorn, but whatever plants are used they should be gathered when they are in the best possible condition. Always collect blossoms and leaves in spring and early summer, fruit and berries in late summer and early autumn, and roots in autumn.

For most recipes the plants may be used fresh or dried. To dry plants, hang them in small bunches or lay them loosely on racks of gauze or sheets of white paper in a warm, dry place. Make sure that there is some flow of air. The temperature should be about 27°C (80°F) for the first 24 hours. Turn them frequently. After a day, reduce the temperature to 21–24°C (70–75°F) and leave them until they are brittle.

Store the dried plants in airtight containers or brown paper bags.

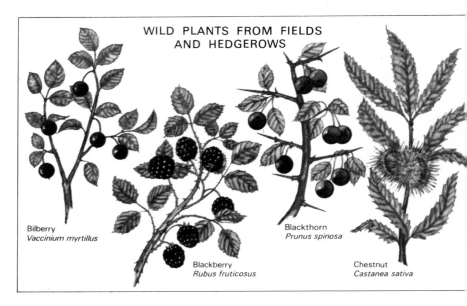

WILD PLANTS FROM FIELDS AND HEDGEROWS

Bilberry
Vaccinium myrtillus

Blackberry
Rubus fruticosus

Blackthorn
Prunus spinosa

Chestnut
Castanea sativa

One of the most common traditional ways to use herbs is to infuse the dried or fresh leaves or flowers in the same way that tea is made.

Crush and bruise the plants so that they can release their juices and pour boiling water over them.

Use three handfuls of fresh plant or one handful of dried plant to each pint of water. Let the infusion steep for at least half an hour, then strain it.

Excessively strong concentrations of herbal tea, or a dosage exceeding a wineglass three times a day can cause a slight temporary indisposition.

After about three days, infusions usually begin to ferment, and should be thrown away.

To get the goodness out of roots, make a decoction by slicing and boiling them for about 20 minutes. Use 1 oz. of dried root or 3 oz. fresh root to a pint of water. Then strain.

To make a herbal syrup, add ½ lb. of honey to 1 pint of a herbal infusion. Boil the mixture over a low heat until it becomes thick.

Recipes for popular British herbs
BLACKBERRY Eat raw or drink an infusion of fresh berries or leaves as a general tonic. The plant's high vitamin C content is beneficial.

BLACKTHORN The soothing syrup that can be made from the fruit or bark is good for coughs. An infusion of the fruit is a gentle laxative and a digestive and liver tonic.

CHESTNUT (sweet) Make a decoction of the bark or nuts, or infuse the leaves to ease irritating coughs.

COWSLIP A few flower heads eaten raw or half a wineglassful of infusion may help sleeplessness.

DANDELION Infused leaves are said to be a kidney tonic. The plant is also a

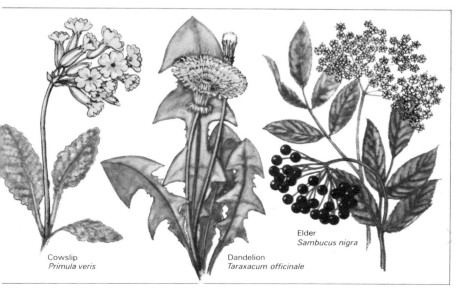

Cowslip
Primula veris

Dandelion
Taraxacum officinale

Elder
Sambucus nigra

laxative and its general cleansing effect helps rheumatics.

ELDER Flowers, leaves and berries can all be used to make infusions for catarrh. Coffeespoon doses can be given safely to small children three times a day. Decoctions of elder root are a general kidney tonic.

FENNEL Infusions of fennel leaves or seeds are good for digestive trouble and act as a mild laxative.

GARLIC Whether raw or cooked, garlic is considered a 'cure-all' herb.

HAWTHORN Infusions of the flowers are recommended for sore throats. It is also possible to add dried leaves to ordinary tea.

MINT Infusions of mint aid digestion and ease nausea.

NETTLES Infusions are a general tonic. The plants may also be eaten as a vegetable (cooked like spinach with a knob of butter, salt and a little water).

PRIMROSE Infusions of the flowers have long been favoured as a pain-killer for rheumaticky joints.

WATERCRESS The iron and vitamins in the plant are good for rheumatics and as a general tonic. It can be eaten raw, or infused.

Herbs for the skin and hair

WILD HERB FACE PACKS Chop the leaves of fresh herbs. Crush them and simmer, in just enough water to prevent burning, for ten minutes until they make a thick mash.

Spread the mixture on to thin muslin and slap it straight on the face. Leave it there for 15 minutes and then remove it and wash your face with water containing a few drops of lemon juice. The treatment will clean and revive tired skin.

A herb face pack can be made from a combination of dandelion leaves,

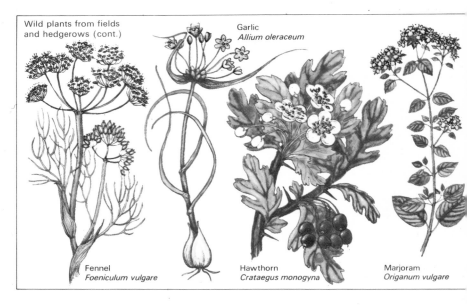

Wild plants from fields and hedgerows (cont.)

Garlic
Allium oleraceum

Fennel
Foeniculum vulgare

Hawthorn
Crataegus monogyna

Marjoram
Origanum vulgare

nettle leaves and elder flowers, all mixed together in equal parts.

WILD HERB BATH MIX Take equal parts of dried dandelion and nettle leaves, and small quantities of the dried roots and flowers of cowslip to make a total of 6 oz. Infuse the herbs in 6 pints of hot water for half an hour. Strain the liquid into a hot bath.

The bath mix soothes and refreshes at the end of a tiring day.

FACE CREAMS Use ordinary cold cream as a base. But because water-based infusions and decoctions do not blend with cold cream, the juices and perfumes of the plants used in a face cream must first be blended into an 'essential oil'.

Pound a handful of elderberries or flowers to make 2 tablespoonfuls. Place the herbs in a mixture of 1 tablespoonful of wine vinegar and ½ pint of corn oil. Pour into a bottle. Steep the herbs for three weeks, shaking the mixture vigorously once a day.

Strain and keep the oil. Repeat the process with the same oil and a new batch of herbs. Repeat until the oil smells quite strongly of the herbs.

Transfer the cold cream into a big pot that will stand in the top of a double saucepan. Put water in the bottom half and heat just a little. Stir in the essential oil gradually, drop by drop, until the cold cream smells strongly of the herb.

HAIR TONICS An infusion of nettle leaves is often used as a tonic to stop dandruff. Rub it into the scalp with the fingertips or rinse the hair (after normal washing) in a pint of it.

For dry hair make a little 'essential oil' (see Face Creams) of nettle leaves and fennel seeds, singly or together. Rub the oil into the scalp and then rinse in clean, warm water.

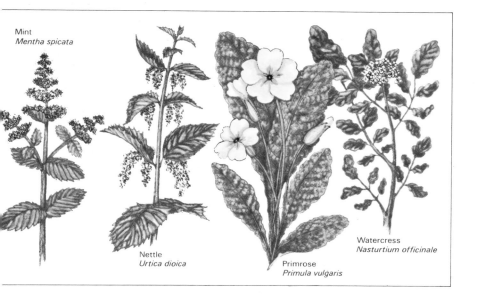

Mint
Mentha spicata

Nettle
Urtica dioica

Primrose
Primula vulgaris

Watercress
Nasturtium officinale

Baskets from British willow

Basket making is one of the oldest and most widespread crafts on earth. In the more than 9000 years that the technique is known to have developed, different races have used basketwork to make walls, doors and roofs of houses. It has been used as rafts and sails, as fish traps and nets, and even had religious significance when primitive peoples made their ceremonial bowls out of basketwork.

Many attempts have been made in recent times, particularly during this century, to perfect basket-making machinery. No satisfactory automatic system has yet been found and true basketry is still a skilled handicraft.

It is remarkable that many of the techniques used by the modern crafts-

A bread basket is a simple example of a 9000-year-old craft. Almost all baskets are still made by hand – no machine has yet been invented to do the job as well

men are similar to those developed and passed on by our ancient forbears many thousands of years before the birth of Christ.

Many grasses, rushes, canes and other materials have been used throughout the world to make baskets, but in Britain by far the most common material is withy or osier willow.

Most of the British willow is grown in Somerset but there are plantations in the north of England, the Midlands and in Essex. To find the nearest source of supply contact a local handicraft dealer.

New osier beds are started with cuttings, planted about 15,000 to the acre. After three years they are cut back to stimulate growth and in the following years the shoots are cut and stacked in bundles called 'bolts'. An osier plantation will produce an annual crop of shoots, or rods, for 30-50 years.

Three grades are usually available. Cheap baskets can be made of green rods which have been cut when they were not in perfect condition. Brown rods, on the other hand, are cut during winter and stored for later use. The third and best grade – white rods – are cut when the sap is still rising in the plant, and they are stacked in water to keep them supple. Finally, before they are used, the bark is normally peeled from them.

Rods are sold by standard lengths, and each length has had a traditional name in the trade which is still sometimes used. The main lengths are: 3 ft (Tacks); 4 ft (Short-Small); 5 ft (Long-Small); and 6 ft (Threepenny). Very short rods, down to 18 in., can also be bought.

Before they are used, the rods must be soaked in water to make them

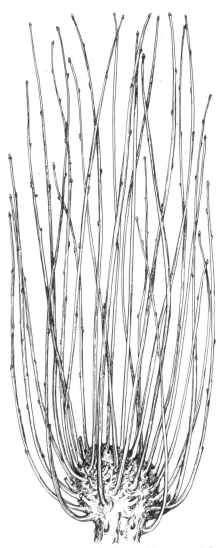

The most common basket-making material in Britain is the withy or osier willow which grows mainly in Somerset. There are three grades – the best are called white rods

pliable. The soaking period depends on the length and type of rod. Very short white rods will need only 15 minutes, while 6 ft white rods will need to be left in the water overnight. After soaking, the rods are stood on their butt ends away from wind and sun, and drained for half an hour. They are then laid down and covered with damp, but not wet, sacking for one to six hours, depending on length.

When they are ready for use the rods will feel barely damp, and smooth. If they are greasy or show mildew, they have probably been left too long under the sacking and must be washed individually and again drained on their butt ends.

While you are working, the unused rods should be kept under the sacking, out of draughts and direct sunlight.

The main tools in basket making

A WILLOW BREAD BASKET—IN 16 STEPS

Tools: shears; knife; bodkin; round-nosed pliers
Materials: about 35 willow rods to make a basket.

Making the base

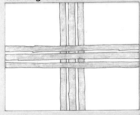

1 Cut six 12 in. lengths from the stout end of the osier willow. Lay them in threes in the form of a cross

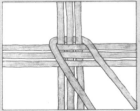

2 Bend a long piece of willow into a U-shape. Hold the cross in one hand and slip the U-shape, called the weaver, over the top arm

3 Twist the left-hand leg of the weaver over the right leg of the weaver and bend it down behind the right arm of the cross

4 Turn the cross 90 degrees to the left so that the right-hand arm becomes the top arm. Twist the new left-hand leg of the weaver over the right weaver and down behind the new right arm of the cross

5 Continue turning the cross to the left, twisting—known as pairing—the weaver for two complete rounds

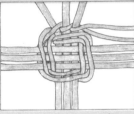

6 Separate the individual willow pieces of the cross and bend them slightly upwards. Continue pairing the weavers round each willow. While pairing, gradually mould the base into a 'dished' shape

Fitting new weavers

7 When a new length of weaver is needed, push it in behind the end of the one that has been used. If the end of the old willow is thick, push in the thin end of the new rod. If the old one is thin, push in the new thick end

are the weaver's own hands, but four implements are also essential: basket-making shears (or secateurs); a sharp knife (which must be kept sharp constantly); a bodkin for opening up a path through the work for the new rod; and a pair of round-nosed pliers for pulling rods through.

Although many shapes, sizes and designs are possible in basketwork, the beginner should experiment first with a simple basic design – for example, a round or oval bread basket.

The foundation of the basket is a base – called the slath – which is made by using a weaving technique called pairing.

When the bottom of the basket is complete, upright pieces of willow – called stakes – are inserted, and the willow that makes up the side or wall of the basket is built up around them.

8 Stop weaving when the base is the size required for the basket being made. Trim the ends of the willows that made the original cross, but make sure that the two weavers still have a workable length

Making the sides

9 Cut 24 pieces of willow about 12 in. long and cut a slanting piece off one side of the thick end of each

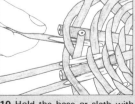

10 Hold the base or slath with the crown shape upwards and slip the cut ends of the willows into the weave on each side of the original base stakes. Push them in about 2½ in.

11 Place the base on a flat surface and bend the 24 side stakes upright. Tie them all loosely at the top to maintain the shape

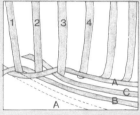

12 Add a third weaver to the two you already have from the pairing weave. Push a new willow (C) into the space between the uprights in front of the existing two weavers (A and B). Take A in front of two uprights, behind the third and in front of the fourth

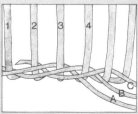

13 Do the same with B and C. Continue this new weaving pro-

cess, called waling, for three complete rounds

14 Trim the end of one of the weavers and then resume pairing with the two remaining willows. Add new weavers as needed to reach the height required for the bread basket

15 On the last row, push the ends of the two weavers down into the side of the basket as close as possible to one of the upright willows

Finishing the border

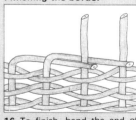

16 To finish, bend the end of each upright behind the one to the right of it and in front of the next. Trim the excess neatly. Trim the ends of any protruding willows on the base or sides

Rushes: The age-old carpet

Throughout the world, rushes have long been used as a craft material. In Saxon times in England, they were simply strewn over the floors of cottages, halls, inns and castles as a loose, primitive form of carpet. When the carpeting needed to be renewed the old rushes were thrown away and

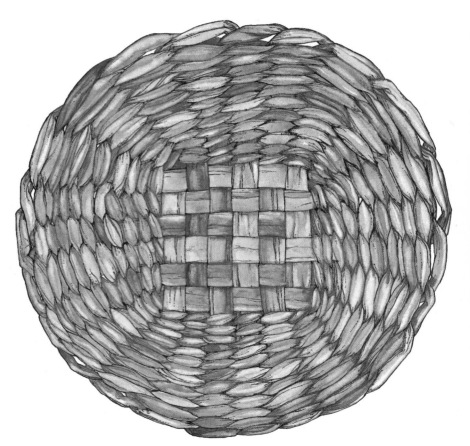

A table-mat is an easy type of rushwork for a beginner, but down the ages rushes have been used for carpeting, basket making and for making slippers. Rushlights – a rush dipped in fat – were the common form of lighting in poor homes for centuries

new rushes were cut and laid down.

At about the same time, rushes dipped into fat or grease were burnt to give light.

In the Middle Ages, rushwork became an established craft, and the rushes were woven to form carpets and baskets.

Modern rushwork has taken on a completely different look, but the techniques involved are no more difficult than those used in earliest times. The present-day craftsman uses rushes to make table-mats, floor-mats, plant holders, work baskets and even the soles of slippers.

Britain's most common rush is the flowering rush *(Juncus effusus)*. It is found in many parts of the country – wherever there is marshy land or water – and is most common by the edge of slow-flowing rivers and streams and around lakes and ponds. (If there is no convenient supply of rushes they can usually be obtained through a handicraft dealer.)

Rushes should always be cut as close as possible to the roots. Keep the cut stems as straight as possible and tie them into armful-sized bundles, called bolts. Store the bolts upright, preferably under cover, where the wind can blow through them to dry them quickly. Drying will take anything from three days to a fortnight, depending on the weather.

When rushes are affected by rain or dampness during the drying period, they become blotchy and less attractive for craftwork. Never store them in strong light, which bleaches them. Always draw the rushes that are to be used from the bundle by the thick or butt end. Before they are used for weaving, however, they must be damp.

Lay them on a flat surface – such as

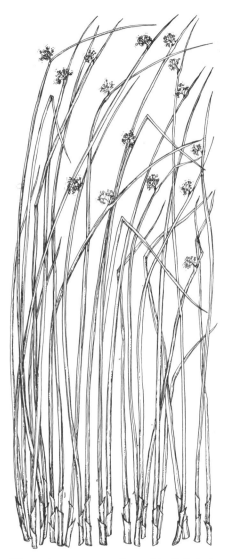

The rush most commonly used in Britain is the flowering rush Juncus effusus, *found by slow-moving rivers and lakes. It should be cut as close as possible to the roots*

a lawn or a driveway – or in a bath, and water them liberally with a watering can. Make sure that the surface water can drain away easily and turn them several times during watering, to ensure that they are dampened evenly. After watering, roll the rushes in a piece of damp blanket or hessian and leave them to 'cure' for about four hours before use.

After about 48 hours, if they are not used, rushes become sticky and must

BASIC RUSHWORK: A ROUND TABLE-MAT

Tools: threading needles (heat and straighten the curved end of a large sacking needle and fix it into a wooden handle. If no sacking needle is available the tool which is used to lace footballs is an excellent substitute); string; scissors; ruler; wooden mallet; brick; towels and cloths; large sheet of polythene
Materials: about 24 rushes to make a mat of about 8 in. in diameter

1 Cover a table with a sheet of polythene and lay a damp cloth over the polythene

Making the centre
2 Cut 12 spokes from the butt (thick) end of the rushes. Lay six spokes close together so that the thicker end of each is alongside the thinner end of the spoke next to it

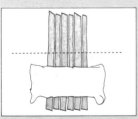

3 Cover a brick with cloth and lay it across the rushes, three spoke thicknesses towards you from an imaginary centre line

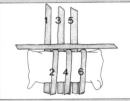

4 Lift spokes 2, 4 and 6 over the brick and lay a new spoke across 1, 3 and 5

5 Flatten spokes 2, 4 and 6 on top of the new spoke

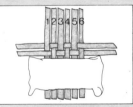

6 Lift spokes 1, 3 and 5 and lay a new spoke over 2, 4 and 6. Flatten 1, 3 and 5

7 Weave in the four remaining cut spokes in the same way and in the same order

Weaving the mat
8 Move the cloth-covered brick to the top edge of the centre weave, which is called the check weave, and select a long thin weaver rush

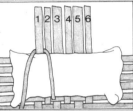

9 Loop one-third of the rush's length back into a hairpin shape and hook it firmly round spoke number 1

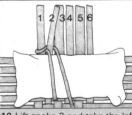

10 Lift spoke 2 and take the left leg of the hairpin shape across spoke 1, behind 2 and down over the brick

11 Press down spoke 2 and lift spoke 3. Take the new left leg of the hairpin shape over 2, behind 3 and down over the brick. When spoke 6 has been

be dried. If this happens they must be dampened again before use.

The simplest form of rushwork for a beginner is a table-mat – either round or oval. In both cases the work starts with a chequer-board pattern of inter-twined rushes. The only significant difference in technique between oval and round mats is that the oval starts with a rectangular centre pattern whereas the round type requires a square centre.

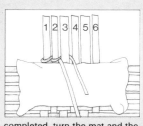

completed, turn the mat and the brick 90 degrees around to the left, and then continue weaving the rush through the next six spokes

12 Continue this operation, called the pairing weave, until the mat is about 8 in. in width

Starting a new weaver

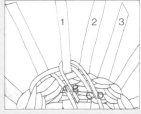

13 When only about 4 in. of a weaver is left, push 4 in. of the tip of a new rush behind the last spoke used. Bend the tip round the spoke

14 To continue pairing, hold the short end of the new rush (B) with the longer end of weaver (A). Take the two together across spoke 1, behind 2 and in front of 3

15 Take the short end of the old rush (C) and the new weaver (D) in front of 2, behind 3 and in front of 4. Continue weaving until only about 1 in. of both short ends is left. Make sure that the excess is on the underside of the mat

Finishing the weave
16 When the mat has reached the required width, turn it over and take the ends of both weavers to the underside

17 Find the spoke closest to the end of one weaver. Push a threading needle in from the edge of the mat, on top of that spoke and under four rows of the weave

18 Thread the end of the weaver rush into the needle and pull it gently through under the four rows of weave

19 Repeat that operation with the end of the second weaver. Trim the ends of all weavers left on the underside

Making a border
20 Start at any position on the mat. Push the threading needle

under four rows of weave on top of a spoke

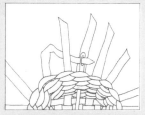

21 Take the spoke second on the left from the needle. Bring it behind the spoke next to the needle, thread it into the needle and pull the spoke through the four rows of weave

22 Continue the operation until all the spokes are used. Trim all the ends

Making an oval mat
Only the centre weave of an oval mat is different in technique from a round mat

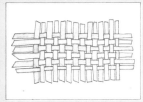

Cut 20 spokes. Lay 14 side by side and use two covered bricks to hold them firmly while the remaining six spokes are woven into them

Spinning and dyeing wool

Wherever there are sheep, there is fleece that can be gathered, spun into yarn and knitted into garments or woven into rugs. Sheep shed their fleeces in early summer – on hedges, fences or on the ground. It is always advisable to seek permission from a farmer before gathering wool on his land.

When gathering fleece, remove any grass, twigs or dirt. Do not collect fleece that looks grey and dry and whose fibres break if pulled; it was probably shed the previous year.

The most primitive form of spinning is with a simple home-made spindle. The yarn may break at first and be full of lumps, but when it is knitted, the uneven texture adds interest, and

SPINNING—AS IT WAS DONE FOR CENTURIES

Tools: sharp knife
Materials: $\frac{3}{8}$ in. dowelling; $\frac{1}{2}$ in. thick wood disc; wool fleece

Making the spindle
1 Cut a piece of $\frac{3}{8}$ in. dowelling, 12–14 in. long

2 Cut a wooden disc about 3 in. in diameter and about $\frac{1}{2}$ in. thick with a $\frac{3}{8}$ in. hole in the centre (or one half of a large apple will do as a temporary measure)

3 Push the dowel through the disc or the apple so that about $\frac{3}{4}$ in. protrudes

4 Cut a notch sloping upwards about $\frac{3}{4}$ in. from the other end of the stick

Spinning
5 The first step in spinning is to take a handful of fleece in one hand and pull out a few fibres with the other. Twist them clockwise as they are pulled out of the fleece ball

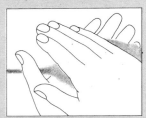

6 When working alone hook the beginning of the yarn on to a sharp object so that it is held firmly. Do not overstretch the wool, but continue pulling and rolling the fibres between the palms of the hands. Always twist the wool in the same direction. And if a helper is holding the end of the yarn he should also twist, but in the opposite direction

7 When about 18 in. of yarn has been spun, tie it to the spindle just above the disc. Take it down over the disc, around the stick below it and loop it round the

notch at the top of the spindle with a half-hitch

8 Hold the ball of fleece in the left hand and overlap several

it is highly prized by handweavers.

Having spun the wool, there is no finer way to dye it than to use the subtle colours of wild plants and berries.

Some dyestuffs – for example, lichens and walnuts – can be used directly on wool; other plants require the wool to be prepared so that it can absorb the colour. This process is called 'mordanting' and it is vital.

The most usual mordants are alum and cream of tartar, obtainable from a chemist. Other mordants known as iron (ferrous sulphate), tin (stannous chloride) and chrome (bichromate of potash) are only available from chemical suppliers. Always keep mordants out of the reach of children.

Different mordants produce different shades with the same dyestuff. For example, tin usually brightens a colour, iron darkens it, and chrome gives strong tones to yellow dyes.

Recipes for mordants

ALUM 3–4 oz. alum, 1 oz. cream of tartar, 1 lb. wool, large pan, cold water.

inches of the yarn with wool fibres. Now hold them firmly together between the left thumb and forefinger

9 Twist the spindle sharply clockwise with the right hand. Keep it clear of the ground. (It is best to stand up while you are using the spindle)

10 When the twist in the wool has run up and joined the fibres and thread together, move the

right thumb and forefinger up to within ½ in. of the left, and hold on while the spindle is still turning clockwise

11 Slacken the left hand just enough to release more of the fibres and pull them upwards from the right hand's grasp. The spindle should still be turning clockwise

12 Take away the right hand so that the new fibres can be taken up with the rising twist. Keep the spindle rotating with the right hand. The spinning sequence is: Spin (right hand); Hold (right hand); Pull (left hand); Release (right hand). The rising twist can be felt when it reaches up to the right hand. This is the precise moment to release more of the fibres from the left hand and let go with the right hand

13 Continue in this way to the extent of the reach of your left arm, then unhitch the yarn from top and bottom of the spindle and wind it round the stick, criss-cross up and down, to form a cone shape. (This keeps the spindle properly balanced.) Leave about 18 in. of the yarn

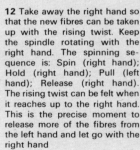

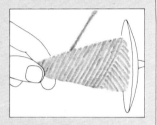

unwound for when you start spinning again

14 When the spindle is full (do not overload), wind the yarn off the spindle into a ball, leaving the last 18 in. of yarn to start spinning again

Washing the wool

1 Wind the wool removed from the spindle into a skein. Tie loosely in four places

2 Prepare a bowl of hot water and a lather of pure soap. Soak the wool for about 20 minutes and then wash it out gently but thoroughly. Do not wring or twist

3 Rinse in warm water, with a little ammonia

4 Spin dry

Dissolve the alum and cream of tartar separately and add to the pan of water – up to 3 gallons. Always make sure the mordant is completely dissolved. Heat the water until tepid and add up to 1 lb. of wetted wool. Bring the water gradually to boiling point in not less than one hour. Make sure it is boiling thoroughly, then reduce the heat and simmer for a further 45 minutes. Stir gently once or twice. Lift out the wool and drain it. Do not wring or squeeze. It may be dyed immediately or left wrapped in a cloth for several days.

TIN $\frac{1}{2}$ oz. stannous chloride, 2 oz. cream of tartar, 1 lb. wool. Process as alum.

CHROME $\frac{1}{4}$–$\frac{1}{2}$ oz. bichromate of potash, 1 lb. wool. Keep a lid on the pan during mordanting as chrome is sensitive to light. Wash wool and dry in shade if not dyed immediately.

IRON $\frac{1}{2}$ oz. ferrous sulphate, 1 oz. cream of tartar, 1 lb. wool. Unlike other mordants, iron should be used only after wool has been boiled with the dyestuff for 30 minutes. Lift out wool, add thoroughly dissolved mordants (separately), replace the wool and boil for a further 30 minutes.

Choosing natural dyes

Particular plants will provide certain ranges of colour, but when dyeing it is best not to plan on a precise shade. The final result will vary with each batch. The delight of natural dyeing lies in the original shades that it produces.

The harder the materials used the longer it takes to bring out the colour. Bark should be soaked in cold water for a couple of days before the process starts, while soft berries give out their colour very quickly.

The general rule for dyeing is to put the dyestuff (at least 1 lb. to 1 lb. of wool) into cold water, bring it slowly to the boil and continue to boil until the colour is given off (only seconds for soft berries; two or three hours for bark). The liquid is left to cool; the wool is put in, brought slowly to the boil and simmered until a good colour

---

CAPTURING THE COLOUR OF NATURAL DYES

Tools: large pan or bucket made of aluminium, galvanised iron or enamel; scissors; muslin; smooth wooden sticks; rubber gloves
Materials: dyestuff

1 Cut up large dyestuff with scissors. Place dyestuff in a pan of cold water and bring slowly to the boil. Boil for the time required by the particular dyestuff (see p. 37)

2 Leave to cool until it is tepid

3 Put in the wool. If the dyestuff consists of loose twigs, or small pieces of bark, separate it from the wool with a layer of muslin. Bring the dye slowly to the boil again and simmer

4 Stir the wool occasionally with a smooth stick. Make sure that the stick is not badly stained from a previous dyeing as it can spoil the colour

5 Simmer the wool in the dye until a good colour is achieved. Remember that the wool looks darker when wet and unwashed

6 Put on rubber gloves, lift out the wool with the stick and gently squeeze

7 Rinse the wool thoroughly in running water

8 Dry in an airing cupboard

The natural dyes of the countryside give beautifully subtle colours to wool, whether hand-spun or bought undyed from a shop. The buds of bracken give yellow and olive shades; blackberries give a slate blue; and elder leaves give various shades of green

is achieved. The wool is removed, gently squeezed out, rinsed thoroughly in cold water and dried. The colour should then be fast.

Recipes for dyes

APPLE OR ASH BARK Mordant: Alum (gives yellows and olives). Boil at least 2 hours before adding wool.

BILBERRIES No mordant (slate blue). Use 1 lb. well-bruised berries to 1 lb. wool. Boil for just a few seconds before adding wool.

BIRCH BARK Mordant: Alum (fawns) or iron (purple). Boil at least 2 hours before adding wool.

BLACKBERRIES Mordant: Alum plus 1 oz. salt to 1 lb. of berries (slate blue). Crush the berries into cold water, boil for a few seconds, then cool. Strain out seeds before adding wool.

BRACKEN BUDS Mordant: Alum (yellowish-green). Simmer for 2 hours before adding wool.

ELDER LEAVES Mordant: Alum for yellowish-green; alum plus a tablespoonful of salt for blue. Boil about an hour before adding wool.

ELDER BARK Mordant: Iron (black). Boil for 2 hours before adding wool.

GOLDEN ROD Mordant: Chrome, plus 2 oz. cream of tartar (golden-yellow). Simmer 2–3 hours before adding wool.

LICHEN (BLACK CROTTLE) No mordant (rust, orange, brown, copper). Simmer for 2-3 hours before adding wool.

LING (HEATHER) Mordant: Alum (yellow). Use 2 lb. to 1 lb. of wool. Simmer 3-4 hours before adding wool.

PRIVET LEAVES Mordant: Alum (yellow). Boil for about an hour before adding wool.

WALNUTS No mordant (dark brown and black). Soak the whole fruit – ripe or unripe – for several days first. Boil for $\frac{1}{2}$ hour before adding wool.

The beauty of sea-shells

Britain's coastline has very many different kinds, shapes and sizes of shells. The most common are mussels, winkles and cockles, but even they present an almost infinite variety.

One of the most attractive shells is the scallop, which ranges in colour from cream to pink-yellow and brown. Some are almost black. Scallop shells may be about the size of a little fingernail or several inches wide.

Always wash shells thoroughly to remove loose sand and any salty deposits. If salt is left on the shells, patches of damp tend to appear on them in wet weather.

When shells are to be kept for some time it helps to sort them by type and size, so that when some are wanted later the whole collection does not have to be upset.

Shell pictures

Shells can be used to create some unusual collage pictures. Cut a piece of hardboard or plywood to a suitable size for hanging the picture.

Select the shells to be included and lay them out on a flat surface alongside the backing board. Arrange them until a satisfactory design is achieved.

MAKING A LAMP WITH SCALLOP SHELLS

Tools: drill and ¼ in. bit; sharp knife; old kitchen knife; electrical screwdriver

Materials: wine bottle; lampholder socket; 5 ft flexible wiring; Polyfilla; selection of shells; plug; 60 watt bulb; lampshade

1 Choose a suitable wine bottle. Wash it thoroughly and remove the label

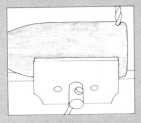

2 Hold the wine bottle carefully in a vice and drill a ¼ in.

diameter hole in the side, just above the base

3 Thread a length of electric flex through the hole and feed it up through the bottle. Connect it to a lampholder socket at the neck of the bottle. Fix the socket in the neck

4 Choose enough small attractive shells to cover the whole surface area of the bottle. Make sure that there are enough shells of an even smaller size to fit around the narrow neck. Wash the shells thoroughly to remove any sand or salt. Salt deposits will cause damp patches to occur in wet weather

5 Use an old kitchen knife to coat the bottle with a thick Polyfilla mixture, and press on the shells while it is still moist. Allow to dry overnight

6 Trim any excess Polyfilla with a sharp knife when the shells are firmly set in position

7 Fit a plug to the flex. Fit a lampshade and 60 watt bulb

Scallop shells range in colour from cream to almost black, and from fingernail size to hand size. They can be used to make shell pictures, jewellery and even lamp-stands

Squeeze a little PVA adhesive, such as Multiglue, Unibond or Bondcrete, along the edges of the smaller shells and press them gently but firmly on to the board.

When a shell is more than $1\frac{1}{2}$ in. wide, prepare a pad of tissue paper or cotton wool and glue it inside the shell. Apply adhesive to the outside of the pad and to the edges of the shell and stick it in position on the board.

Jewellery from shells

The smallest and most delicate scallop shells can readily be made into unusual natural jewellery.

EARRINGS Buy a pair of earring mounts (obtainable at craft shops and many large department stores). If possible find or buy two old discarded imitation pearls – perhaps pearls saved from a broken necklace.

Choose two small scallop shells, and wash and dry them thoroughly. Use PVA adhesive to stick a pearl into the centre of each shell. When the cement is set, stick the back of each scallop shell on to an earring mount.

NECKLACE Select as many scallop shells as are needed to make a necklace. Lay them out so that there is a single large shell in the middle and make sure that the sizes gradually reduce towards the ends of the line. Use a small drill to make holes through the top of each shell.

Because scallop shells are brittle, it is usually necessary to have a good stock in reserve to replace shells that get broken.

Fix imitation pearls to the drilled shells and thread them in order on stout linen thread.

A necklace clasp set can be obtained from a craft shop or department store and fixed to the ends of the thread.

True colours of stone

The glistening lustre of a wet pebble dries away all too soon when the stone is taken from the bed of a clear country stream or seaside rock pool. Yet that glossy sparkle can be captured forever by even the most inexperienced beginner in stone polishing.

Rocks that were formed some 2000–

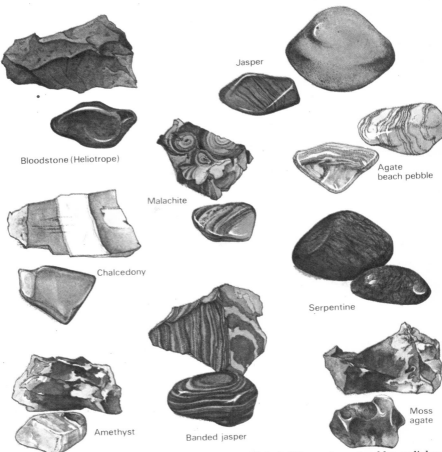

Jasper

Bloodstone (Heliotrope)

Agate beach pebble

Malachite

Chalcedony

Serpentine

Amethyst

Banded jasper

Moss agate

Rough stones found at the seaside, or in rivers or near quarries, can be polished to a high brilliance in a tumbler polisher, and then mounted in jewellery fittings

3000 million years ago and thrust up from the deep layers of the earth are gradually given a natural beauty by centuries of polishing and smoothing in sea and river. With patience and a little effort the home-craftsman can produce this work of nature in only a few days. Tumbler polishers, operated by an electric motor, now make possible a whole range of stonework.

Pieces of rock and rare semi-precious stones that are as old as the countryside itself can be transformed into paperweights, earrings, bracelets, rings or even just a glossy collection to be admired and envied by every

HOW TO USE A TUMBLER POLISHER

Tools: polisher (these instructions are for a machine with two 3 lb. barrels); penknife; hammer; colander; bucket; magnifying glass
Materials: pebbles; silicon carbide grit – coarse grit (60, 80, or 120 mesh) and medium grit (320 or 400 mesh); cerium or tin oxide polishing powder; cork chips; paper or rags for covering rocks being chipped

1 Examine the selected pebbles carefully. If necessary split large specimens with a hammer, but be careful to cover them with cloth or newspaper to avoid injury to the eyes from flying splinters. It is wise to wear goggles while splitting hard rock. If a stone can be scratched with a knife, do not try to tumble polish it (it may be possible to polish it by hand)

2 Load one of the tumbler barrels about three-quarters full with a mixture of small, medium and large stones.

Cover with water and add 2 heaped tablespoonfuls of coarse grit. Fit the lid and press in the centre to squeeze out any air

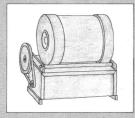

3 Wipe any water from the barrel and place it on the machine, according to the manufacturer's instructions

4 Switch on and leave for 24 hours. Switch off and open the barrel to release any gases. Continue tumbling but release gases every day for about seven days

5 After seven days take out a few stones. Wash and in-

spect them. If they are still rough or scratched continue the tumbling

6 When the stones are smooth, tip them into a colander over a bucket. Wash them under running water

7 Collect the sludge from the bucket and throw it away in a corner of the garden or filter it through rags and put it in the dustbin

8 Wash the pebbles in warm water and detergent. Rinse and dry. Rinse the barrel

9 Replace the stones in the barrel and add water and medium grit. Tumble until they are silky smooth – probably for about nine days. Release the gas once a day

10 Wash and rinse the pebbles and place them in the second barrel. Cover with water and add 1 tablespoonful of polishing powder. Add 2 tablespoonfuls of cork chips or special filler, as a buffer between the stones

11 Tumble for seven days. Release the gas every day

12 When the stones have a high gloss, wash and rinse

GUIDE TO STONES FOR POLISHING

(For tumble polishing, beginners should use stones with a hardness rating above 5)

Stone	Description	Hardness
Topaz	Yellow, pale blue	8
Amethyst	Violet	7
Cairngorm	Golden-brown, transparent	7
Citrine	White with yellow tints or clear yellow	7
Flint	Grey to black	7
Granite	Pink or grey with black and white flecks	7
Jasper	Terracotta-red, green, yellow	7
Quartz	White, cream	7
Rock crystal	Colourless, transparent	7
Rose quartz	Pale pink, glassy	7
Agate	Translucent, light golden-grey (and other colours)	6½
Bloodstone (Heliotrope)	Dark green with red blotches	6½
Carnelian	Flesh red, transparent	6½
Chalcedony	Pale blue-grey or fawn, translucent	6½
Onyx	Black, brown with white bands	6½
Pyrites (Fool's gold)	Brass-gold	6½
Obsidian	Black, glassy	5
Limestone	White, grey to black	4–5 (approx.)
Marble	White, black, grey, green, terracotta	4–5 (approx.)
Fluorspar	Pastel-coloured crystals, transparent	4
Malachite	Green	4
Serpentine	Dark red, mottled green or green, mottled red	4
Slate	Red, green, grey or black	3–4 (approx.)
Jet	Black	3½
Chalk	White	3
Amber	Yellow to reddish-orange	2

visitor. The suitability of a stone for polishing depends on its hardness, measured by scientists on a scale devised by a German mineralogist, Friedrich Mohs.

The hardest mineral in the world, diamond, is given the rating 10. At the other end of the scale, the softest mineral, talc, is rated 1. By comparison, a fingernail would rate 2½, a coin 3 and a penknife blade 6. It is with such everyday items that the amateur can test the rock or pebble that he wants to polish.

Some stones are too soft for the harsh treatment of a tumbler polisher but may be polished by hand. Beginners should not attempt to tumble-polish stones with a rating below 6 (any stone that can be scratched with a knife). The very soft types – such as some limestones – cannot be successfully treated even by hand. But they may nevertheless make attractive decorations in their natural state.

Specimens of every rock found in Britain are on display in the Geological Museum, Exhibition Road, London SW7. The collection provides a unique means of identifying any find that is out of the ordinary.

Remember that all land in Britain –

TURNING STONES INTO JEWELLERY

Tools: jeweller's pliers (snipe-nosed and flat-nosed); wooden skewer, orange stick or tooth-pick ·

Materials: silicon carbide stick or wet-and-dry silicon carbide paper; clean paper; plasticine; 5-minute epoxy resin adhesive; the appropriate type of jewellery fitting; matching stones

1 Wash, rinse and dry the stones. Do not handle areas to be glued

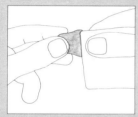

2 Roughen the reverse side of each stone with the silicon carbide stick or wet-and-dry silicon carbide paper

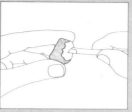

3 Prepare a small amount of epoxy-resin adhesive. Use a skewer, orange stick or tooth-pick to spread it thinly on the roughened area of each of the stones and on the jewellery fitting

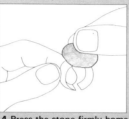

4 Press the stone firmly home and remove surplus glue. Re-peat with other stones and leave them until the adhesive hardens

Drop fittings

Choose pointed stones and roughen their narrow ends. Stand the stones in plasticine with the roughened ends uppermost. Mix the adhesive and apply to a stone and the fittings. Press the fitting on to the stone while it is still in the plasticine. Repeat with the other stones. When the adhesive has hardened fix the fitted stones to a chain

and anything on the land – belongs to someone. Only the landowner has the absolute right to collect pebbles and stones. Although few people complain about modest pebble-gathering, it is advisable to seek permission before trying to find stones on private land.

Polishing the stones

Tumbler polishers are machines which grind the surface of stones with silicone carbide grit. They are available from craft and rock shops. Although some have useful refinements – for example, adjustable speed control – a simple machine polishes just as well.

Make sure that the machine is correctly wired and connected to the power supply. Always stand it on a fireproof base and keep it in a room or building out of earshot. Tumble-polishing, which must be continued day and night for more than two weeks, is fairly noisy.

A beginner should use only hard stones that cannot be scratched with a knife. With experience it is possible to polish some of the softest types by varying the time allowed for each stage in the machine.

HAND POLISHING When a pebble is too large or too soft for the tumbler polisher, hand polishing is a useful, if somewhat slower, method.

A kit, which can be bought at a craft or rock shop, consists of coarse, medium, and fine silicon carbide grit, and polishing powder, usually tin or cerium oxide.

Have available a spoon, a small brush and old cup. With round stones, use a bowl; for flat stones, a piece of plate glass. For the polishing stage, a hand buff of wood covered with un-dyed leather or felt is suitable.

Add water to coarse grit to form a thick slurry. Rub the pebble or rock in the mixture from side to side and round and round the bowl or glass, so that all the surfaces are gradually ground smooth. When the rough and scratched areas are even, wash and clear away the coarse grit.

Repeat with medium grit to smooth the pebble still further. When it is satisfactory, clear away the medium grit. Repeat with fine grit, then wash off every trace of the silicon carbide.

Put some polishing powder in a cup and mix with water to a thick paste. Brush on to the polishing buff. Polish the pebble or rock until a high gloss is achieved.

Making stone jewellery
Stones polished in their natural ir-regular shape are called 'baroques'. Shaped, domed and rounded stones are 'cabochons' and stones ground with flat faces are 'faceted'.

For most jewellery, cabochons and faceted stones are required. They and the ready-made jewellery fittings that are used can be bought from a rock or craft shop, but it is possible also to prepare these stones at home on a special lapidary machine.

The machine, which costs at least

£30 plus the price of the motor, usually has several grinding, sanding and polishing wheels. A diamond-grit saw blade enables stones to be cut or trimmed to shape.

If a lapidary machine is not avail-able, choose small polished stones that are naturally suitable for the jewellery that is to be made. In most cases, when matching stones are needed, they must be bought.

Many types of jewellery – rings, pendants, earrings, bracelets and necklaces – can be made.

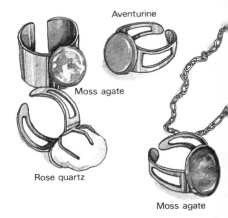

Aventurine

Moss agate

Rose quartz

Moss agate

Bloodstone (Heliotrope)

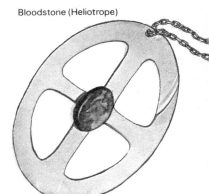

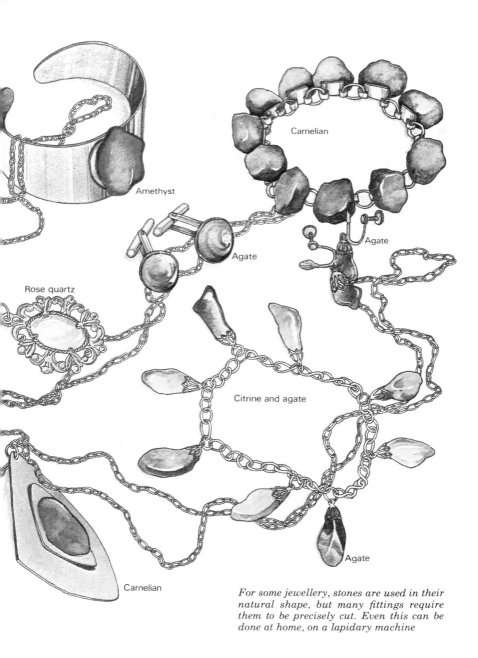

Amethyst

Carnelian

Agate

Agate

Rose quartz

Citrine and agate

Carnelian

Agate

For some jewellery, stones are used in their natural shape, but many fittings require them to be precisely cut. Even this can be done at home, on a lapidary machine

Brass portraits of chivalry

More than 4000 monumental brasses, dating from as early as 1300, still exist in British churches. (A complete catalogue, published by the Victoria and Albert Museum, London, is obtainable at most bookshops.)

These brasses – engraved sheets set in stone slabs – were laid as memorials over tombs, to represent and commemorate the dead who lie beneath – knights, merchants, ladies, priests and even children. Their designs and accompanying inscriptions are a fascinating record of history and fashion.

The origin of monumental brasses goes back to the 12th century, when it was becoming common practice to commemorate the dead with sculptured figures and engraved stone. Brass work was used to decorate engraved stone memorials, and eventually complete brass plates became a convenient alternative, as they could be set flat in the floor.

Making a rubbing is easy. The basic materials – architects' white detail paper and black heel ball – are cheap, and the results are decorative, unusual and interesting.

Always obtain permission from the vicar or verger before starting to rub. Most churches charge a fee that ranges from a few pence to several pounds, depending on the condition and importance of the brass. A usual fee would be £1 per rubbing.

Take care never to damage the

Monumental brasses are a valuable record of fashion and customs. This rubbing – of Sir Walter Fitzralph who died in 1323 – was taken at Pebmarsh church in Essex

brasses or the church in any way, and always have respect for worshippers in the church.

Brasses are sometimes protected by a mat, but church brochures generally say where they can be found.

To achieve more spectacular rubbings, use gold or silver heel ball on black paper or on coloured book binders' linen. Gold and silver heel ball are rather soft and it is easy to make mistakes with them, so work carefully. The gold rubbings can be finished off at home with 'Goldfinger' wax gilding paste.

Brown or white heel ball gives good rubbings on gold or dark papers respectively, and children's coloured crayons, although a little soft, are effective to pick out details of heraldry or dress.

Use black plastic poster hangers to hang finished rubbings. Small rubbings can be framed.

THE ART OF BRASS RUBBING

Tools: small soft brush; soft duster; cardboard tubes (from a draper)

Materials (obtainable from art shops): architects' white detail paper in several widths (plain wallpapers can be used for narrow brasses); black heel ball; 'Acorn' crayons (thick and thin); plastic eraser; masking tape

1 Clean away all dust with a soft brush or duster. Study the brass and memorise or make a note of all its parts. Once the paper is down, it cannot be lifted until the rubbing is finished

2 Lay the paper squarely over the brass, with 1 ft overlap top and bottom. Stick the paper to the stone surround or 'matrix' with pieces of mask-

ing tape. Never use ordinary clear adhesive tape as it damages both the paper and the stone

3 Feel around the edges of the brass with the fingers and press down the paper to mark the outlines

4 Take a piece of heel ball firmly in one hand. Grip it across the palm with all fingers, not like a pencil

5 Hold the paper steady with the other hand and start rubbing a few inches in from one edge. Make short hard strokes across the paper

6 Take care not to go over the edges. Work until the whole brass is covered, making strokes in all directions so

that individual strokes do not show and the image is good and black. Make sure that every detail has been well rubbed. Always use a duster to flick away loose pieces of heel ball.

Take care not to tear the paper around protruding rivets or damaged brass

7 Take off the tape, roll up the rubbing and put it into a cardboard tube

8 Lay the rubbing on a smooth wooden table and touch in any bad spots and blemishes with a crayon

9 Use a plastic eraser to remove any light heel ball marks beyond the edges of the brass. Heavy mistakes are difficult to shift. It is possible to use white spirit on a clean rag but the paper is generally marked. If necessary, white poster paint can be used on bad mistakes

10 If there is a tear, smooth out the paper and stick it together on the back with clear adhesive tape

*Monumental brass commemorating Elizabeth and Peter Halle (c. 1430)
at Herne in Kent (height 3 ft 6 in.)*

Printing and binding by Varnicoat Ltd, Pershore